Brief Accident of Light

Poems of Newburyport

Brief Accident of Light

Poems of Newburyport

by Rhina P. Espaillat & Alfred Nicol
Illustrations by Kate Sullivan

© 2019 Alfred Nicol, Rhina Espaillat, Kate Sullivan.
All rights reserved.
This material may not be reproduced in any form, published,
reprinted, recorded, performed, broadcast,
rewritten or redistributed without
the explicit permission of Alfred Nicol, Rhina Espaillat,
and Kate Sullivan.
All such actions are strictly prohibited by law.

ISBN: 978-1-950462-32-2
Cover illustration by Kate Sullivan
Cover design by Shay Culligan

Kelsay Books
502 S. 1040 E. A-119
American Fork, Utah 84003
Kelsaybooks.com

Acknowledgments

Our thanks to the following publications, where several of the poems in this manuscript first appeared or are scheduled to appear:

Better Than Starbucks!: "At Dusk," "Oak Hill Cemetery" and "The Youngest Actors Take The Stage"

Light: "Hugo Licked Me"

Think: "Fog at Night," "The Marina in October" and "Wandering City Hall"

Contents

Plum Island Zazen	13
Dawn: Plum Island	14
Waking Up	17
First Stop	19
Morning Railway Riders	21
Playground	22
The Youngest Actors Take the Stage	24
Wandering City Hall	25
Passages: City Hall	27
Fly-By: The Newburyport Art Association	28
Hugo Licked Me	29
On the Promenade	31
Marina Flags	32
The Marina in October	34
The Closing Year	36
Oak Hill Cemetery	38
Reading the Stones: Oak Hill Cemetery	41
At Dusk	43
Nightfall: Plum Island	44
Fog at Night	46

A Note

Brief Accident of Light is a collection of twenty poems, ten by Rhina P. Espaillat and ten by Alfred Nicol. The poems were written for an arts collaboration initiated by Newburyport Chamber Music Festival Director David Yang. Mr. Yang, a distinguished violist and composer, made a list of emblematic locations in and around the city of Newburyport, and assigned to each location a specific time of day or night. He first commissioned composer Robert Bradshaw to write a new piece for string quartet drawing its inpiration from those locations. Mr. Yang then invited Espaillat and Nicol to visit each spot at the specified time and to give voice to their experiences in a series of poems. Because the poets chose to make their visits together, most of the poems gathered here are paired —a reader will hear two voices emanating from each place, as when two birds perch in the same tree.

    The two poets found themselves a little taken aback by the way these poems seemed to write themselves. One can only surmise that the spirits of City Hall and Oak Hill Cemetery really had something they needed to express, and were only waiting for an opportunity! A poet can get carried away when that kind of thing happens. You'll see that there are four unpaired poems in this collection— "Waking Up," "Fly-By: The Newburyport Art Association," "The Closing Year," and "Fog at Night"—each resulting from one or the other poet writing from a place not mentioned on the original list.

    In keeping with the collaborative nature of this project, Kate Sullivan was invited to illustrate the collection with images of the sites mentioned in the poems. She too got caught up in the spirit of Mr. Yang's vision and contributed the celebratory ink-wash sketches the reader will happen upon, turning these pages.

Plum Island Zazen

sitting on the beach at 5:01am

The sea is nowhere to be seen.
Yet all that meets the eye,
near or far, or in-between,
is either sea or sky.

A sliver of moon and one pale star
peer from behind a cloud.
The sea, approaching where we are,
has never been so loud.

Could be its ceaseless restlessness
has tossed the sea all night.
We'll recognize the sea, I guess,
when first we see the light.

AN

Dawn: Plum Island

Sullen, compulsive sea,
why do you threaten me
with foaming lips
and icy fingertips
incessantly?

What can I do
to hide on these bare dunes?
But I have witnesses: the moon's
silver-lidded eye—stars too—
are fixed on you.

And more: a crowd
of gulls shouting out loud
know what you've done.
And look—robed in a cloud,
His Honor, the sun!

RPE

Waking Up

Hysterical gulls
A half-moon in the blue sky
Get over it
.

Resolution tied
to a blue-and-white buoy,
its mooring line slack
.

Fishing boats follow
the bright trail the rising sun
blazes out to sea
.

One glove finger snipped,
the white-haired philosopher
captures Pokémon
.

My wife skimming stones
Children's voices from the boats
across the river
.

A harbor seal's head
pokes out from beneath the yacht's
glossy reflection

Those fucking squirrels
don't see us till the small one
who's on top gets off
.

The cat paws the screen
Outside, the magnolia boughs
weighted with waxwings
.

Leaping the stone wall
a deer then a dog barking
four paws off the ground
.

Steeple on a hill
congregation of tall masts
sheltering below
.

What kind of incense
burns in these cool rooms beneath
the flowering linden?
.

Raindrops on the pond
That girl never says a word
She must be counting
                      AN

First Stop

the MBTA commuter station at 7:30 am

The bells have cleared their throats. The morning train,
which usage has made human, knows the drill.
It rests here while the seats begin to fill.
A red-haired woman steps out of the rain,
and there's her profile in a window-pane.
New faces fill the other frames, until
the bells

convince a young man skateboarding the lane
he could be getting somewhere, sitting still.
And though the engine grumbles, old joints shrill,
once rolling, it remembers its refrain—
the bells

AN

Morning Railway Riders

One glides on swiftly via skateboard.
We Two (like the idle snoops we are!)
people-watch, glad to be ignored,
while Three hunt for the Quiet Car.
Four stride on briskly, briefcase-solemn.
Now little kids scramble on—Five—
with their grownups, a weary column
of Six, all looking half alive.
Seven, Eight, Nine, Ten, make it quick,
before the doors are shut—click click!
Eleven, Twelve…oops, turning back:
too late: we're off, click clack, click clack.

RPE

Playground

Lumpy rocks to climb on;
mud to stomp around;
slides to spend some time on
before you head on down;

twisty tubes to crawl in;
bars to squiggle through;
holes you're not to fall in
until, of course, you do;

playmates to smash into
running at full speed;
fountains to dash into—
a shower's what you need!—

and before you're any wetter,
dash out of right away.
Can anything be better?
It's a perfect day!

RPE

The Youngest Actors Take the Stage

the Inn Street Playground at 11:00 am

Cleopatra in her golden sandals
clambers up the pyramid to spy
on Mark and Toni,

while Mark and Toni, off like Roman candles,
chase another youngster whizzing by—
Oh, that one rides a pony!

No, that one *is* a pony! And this one's wild
to press a fountain back with her bare hands.
Good luck with that!

Good luck with that, and good luck to the child
whose fountain of a pony-tail withstands
her trying on a hat.

She's trying on a hat, and aren't they all?
Here comes Amelia Earhart, who can fly!
There's Errol Flynn!

And Errol Flynn, who's ten feet tall,
larger-than-life where life is but knee-high,
sports a rakish grin.

Flashing that rakish grin, his boots spread wide,
he brandishes his sword over the sea
where tigers swim!

Where *tigers* swim! while, stone-still on the slide,
one toddler waits in vain for gravity
to notice him.   *AN*

Wandering City Hall

More serious than I am, to be sure,
the servicemen portrayed here—commandants,
the naval officer who died in France
of some disease for which we've found the cure,
the Great War vets—all find me immature.
They sum me up with just a passing glance,
and envy me my easy circumstance:
I've only their reproval to endure.

I duck and hurry past them up the stairs.
An empty concert hall, with chandeliers!
There in the balcony, the paint is peeling.
Reflections move across the stucco'd ceiling.
I'll sit awhile. There's nothing more to do.
These silences should count as music, too.

AN

Passages: City Hall

A busy place, where those who come will find
passports and testaments,
and on these broad, high walls, neatly aligned,
our wars: and to record their vast expense,
these faces left behind.

Look at their youthful smiles, helmets and caps
and bygone hairstyles, worn
jauntily, with bravado, before Taps
turned permanent, when further days were torn
from them, by grave mishaps.

As if to map their passages—so brief,
so bravely undertaken—
here are the dates and places where the grief
was hatched that left families, friends, forsaken
and mute with disbelief:

From Picardy, Calais, Bois de Belleau,
that row never came back.
Nor these from Metz, Luzon or Anzio,
those from the Mekong Delta or Iraq,
today or long ago.

Busy, these offices, assigned the care
of residents to come,
for whom they legislate, construct, repair.
But these dead say, *Remember how, for some,
no road leads anywhere.*

RPE

Fly-By: The Newburyport Art Association

It's here that the makers gather
with patience, tools and skill,
to see what those three together
can save from what life will spoil.

They live to snare one passing
brief accident of light,
before the spark goes missing
or hisses to smoke, and out.

Their walls are all shallow windows
framing the dreamt or seen
beyond where vision blunders
and darkness will fall too soon.

Where do they hunt each color?
How do they grow each line?
How do they ambush the killer—
Time—and wrestle the rascal down?

They salvage the blooms we pick.
Though the pickers and makers wilt,
bless the makers and what they make
to stall what they cannot halt.

RPE

Hugo Licked Me

Waterfront Promenade Park (with apologies to Leigh Hunt)

Hugo licked me when we met,
tugging at the leash that held him.
That's a breach of etiquette
I've encountered only seldom.
Portside pets are so well-bred
(No one here will contradict me)
owners follow where they're led—
Hugo licked me

AN

On the Promenade

A memory: one brisk fall day,
my mother, elegant in gray,
though very old, straight as a rod,
went walking on the Promenade.

Widowed, confused, dimly aware
of who I was beside her there,
but fond of mischief, and still pretty.
She loved the river and the city,

seagulls and sailboats skimming by.
That afternoon she caught the eye
of an old fellow, bald and thin,
who gripped his cane and slipped right in

between us, like a trusted friend.
We strolled the boardwalk end to end,
we three, at ease, each way and back,
by the sun-speckled Merrimack.

No word was said, no look exchanged.
But as if they had prearranged
to rendezvous right there, right then,
the next day we were three again.

How lovely, after all these years,
this flirting between two old dears,
I thought, and smiled, turning to see
how flushed and flattered she must be.

"Mama," I said, "you have a beau!
And speechless, you've impressed him so!"
"Nonsense," she snapped, serene and cold.
"He's boring, slow, and much too old."

RPE

Marina Flags

Their stars are faded and their stripes are frayed
as high above the ebbing tide they shiver,
among the masts of a white fleet arrayed
like toys dotting the sparkle of the river.

Here and there a sail glides out to sea,
a fishing boat hums back. The other shore—
Salisbury, I think—so tranquilly
at rest in its green setting—seems no more

than painted canvas in a house at peace.
But elsewhere mines explode and sirens blare
and migrants trudge in files that never cease,
from ruined cities under poisoned air.

Why do these threadbare flags seem different from
those once spread wide to greet the hungry flow,
triumphant, welcoming, beckoning "Come!"
to those with nothing and nowhere to go?

RPE

The Marina in October

The winded sailboats rounded up in port
won't soon be running off somewhere,
their standing masts as bare
as stanchions in the nostril-chilling air.
Racing the waves is youthful sport,
and now the days grow short.

Beyond the bend, the island, like a gate,
stays open to admit the fleet
grown slow in their retreat,
who'll huddle here and shudder in the sleet.
Facing inland now, they wait,
they rest and ruminate,

and as the harbor water lifts and falls,
you feel them breathe, like horses in their stalls.

AN

The Closing Year

Beside the Merrimack, in white,
cocooned from winds they hope to ride,
the huddled boats are sleeping tight,
marooned on stilts above the tide.

Above the streets—Federal, State,
Pleasant and High—four steeples stand,
on guard over the city's fate,
in which they mean to have a hand.

Now autumn's copper days are gone;
the maples and the oaks are bare.
Their branches shiver and put on
the thinnest coat of birdless air.

Squirrel and mouse, each tends his town:
so much to scamper for, to hoard,
to drag high up or wrestle down
for warmth in winter, bed and board.

And on their lawns, now brown and sere,
neighbors look up at clouds that pass,
and then retreat indoors to peer
and mime hellos through double glass.

The river, though, goes where it will.
In every season, swift or slow,
it skirts the shade of silent mills,
mirrors old bridges from below,

lapping, at last, the city's docks
where seagulls cry above the bay,
and ripples back from harbor rocks,
as if to go, as if to stay.

RPE

Oak Hill Cemetery

How well-designed, this plot of land
where sloping paths weave through the laurel.
It must belong to someone grand.

How well laid out, and how well-planned,
city-like, yet wholly rural;
how well-conceived, this plot of land

where elms and lichened sculptures stand
unearthly, silent, upright, moral.
It must belong to someone grand

with legionnaires at his command,
who do his will without demurral.
How well-maintained, this plot of land,

ruled with an impartial hand
that claims the child and spares the squirrel.
Its owner must be rich and grand

to gather so much stillness and
to put an end to every quarrel.
How peaceable, this plot of land.
It must belong to someone grand.

AN

Reading the Stones: Oak Hill Cemetery

Cold in the grip of fall, sudden and sere,
and colder still
before each gently rounded hill,
we read the stones that name the sleepers here.

Some left their names on streets the living know
down to this day;
others on history, to say
that though we play our part, we too will go.

How quietly the trees reach for the sky,
but shade each mound,
just as their hidden roots surround,
cradle, and guard what's left of all who die.

Heart that so strives to beat and beat forever,
learn from this place
to treasure life, but leave with grace
those roots that bind and nothing can quite sever.

RPE

At Dusk

At dusk out on Plum Island, in October,
my friend and I sit on a ridge of sand
that overlooks the sea.
Indulging memory,
a child again, she takes her father's hand.
When she grows tired, he lifts her to his shoulder.

Slowly, now, a darkness fills the hollows.
Splotches of sunset founder in the rills.
Closing her eyes, she sees—
beyond the guava trees
along that inland, homeward path she follows—
La Vega in the shadow of its hills.

As for me, I grip the captain's wheel,
each salt air inhalation like a dram;
my dreams are all about
adventure, setting out—
until I feel myself adrift, off-keel,
and start the long way back to where I am.

We brace ourselves as we descend the dune,
caught up in time, itself a kind of tide,
whose whorls and eddies trace
the stories of a place.
Our footprints will get covered over, soon.
For now, they skirt the beachgrass, side by side.

AN

Nightfall: Plum Island

two spindles of white
water crisscross the wide black
loom of night   they meet

untether   retreat
go slack in a quick never
into forever

followed by the last
and swallowed into moonlit
sand   past another

and another whose
foam feathers fit together
but too late   and then

more again   by twos
silverwhite   rush in and fizz
change is all there is

RPE

Fog at Night

The tide goes out, and out,
leaving the fog behind.

The fog then finds its way
under the Custom House,
lifting it slowly up
and setting it back down,
a little to one side
of where it was before.

The storefronts tilt. Some lanes
narrow, others widen.
The lighthouse turns its shoulder,
shying away, while red brick
buildings shift their weight
from one side to the other,
slowly losing patience.

Beneath a blurry moon,
the fog pulls back from things
it has uprooted, waving
the fingers of one hand,
brushing the weathervanes.

Drops fall from the eaves.

By tomorrow morning,
the sidewalks will have settled,
and chimneys will stand up,
trying out thin shadows
in the tentative new light.

AN

Rhina P. Espaillat, born in the Dominican Republic in 1932, has lived in the U.S. since 1939 and taught English in New York City at the high school level. She has been writing since childhood and has published eight full-length books and three chapbooks, comprising poetry, essays, and short stories in both English and her native Spanish. She has also published work in numerous anthologies and magazines, as well as translations, most notably of Robert Frost into Spanish and St. John of the Cross into English. Her awards include the T. S. Eliot Prize for Poetry, the Richard Wilbur Award, The Nemerov Prize, the May Sarton Award, and several from the Poetry Society of America, the New England Poetry Club, and the Ministry of Culture of the Dominican Republic.

Alfred Nicol's most recent collection of poetry, *Animal Psalms*, was published in 2016 by Able Muse Press. He has published two other collections, *Elegy for Everyone* (2009), and *Winter Light*, which received the 2004 Richard Wilbur Award. His poems have appeared in *Poetry, The New England Review, Dark Horse, First Things, Commonweal, The Formalist, The Hopkins Review, Measure* and elsewhere. His awards include The Daniel Varoujan Award of the New England Poetry Club, The Robert Frost Foundation Poetry Award, and the Willis Barnstone Translation Award. Nicol's poem "Addendum" was included in the 2018 edition of *The Best American Poetry.*

Kate Sullivan likes to fiddle around with music, words, and pictures. Her setting of *Pinocchio* for string quartet, narrator, hammer, chisel, and musical saw was premiered by The Providence Quartet. Her *Sweeney Astray,* for chamber orchestra, tenor and a chorus of trees, tells the medieval Irish tale of a mad king transformed into a bird. Her *Mother's Day Fugue* was premiered by The Kremlin Chamber Orchestra at Carnegie Hall. She has written two picture books, *On Linden Square* (Sleeping Bear Press) and *What Do You Hear?* (Schiffer Publishing). Her paintings are hanging in a number of private collections.

Kelsay Books

www.ingramcontent.com/pod-product-compliance
Lightning Source LLC
Chambersburg PA
CBHW021028090426
42738CB00007B/937